FOUR FIELDS

FOUR FIELDS
poems by Dorinda Wegener

Copyright © July 1, 2024 Dorinda Wegener

No part of this book may be used or performed without written consent of the author, if living, except for critical articles or reviews.

Wegener, Dorinda
1st edition

ISBN: 978-1-949487-24-4
Library of Congress Control Number: 2023945630

Interior design by Hadley Hendrix
Cover design by Joel W. Coggins
Primary Editing by Natasha Kane
Supporting Editing by Ali Shafer

Cover: Alfred Stieglitz. *Georgia O'Keeffe—Hands and Thimble*, 1919. The Art Institute of Chicago. This information, which is available on the object page for each work, is also made available under Creative Commons Zero (CC0).

Trio House Press, Inc.
Minneapolis
www.triohousepress.org

for Scott & Emma

*and in memory of my parents
Dolores Philomena & Donald Thomas Foley
and Nana Egan-Macarelli*

Table of Contents

I.

I Write You with the Intention of Amendment	14
There is a Third Eye to Every Memory: Part I	15
Four Fields	17
The Mother, Bird	18
There is a Third Eye to Every Memory: Part II	19
White Grandfather Feathers and Inner Secondary Bone	21
There is a Third Eye to Every Memory: Part III	22
In the Deep, Deep Woods on a Dark, Dark Night	23
Noun : Adjective : Idiom : Verb	24
Today: Kinetic	25
Next to the Child's Bed, a Gessoed Statue of Some Saint	26

II.

Statue	30
Scene with Apparitions	31
Triptych Depicting an Average Morning, Miracles, and the Corpse	32
In Fief or Fee	34
Out of Eden, From the Amtrak Window	35

Mirror, Mirror	36
Attending	38
Self Portrait with Hand Study and Jung's Word Association Test	39
If Your Family Owned a Mausoleum, then This Poem Would Make More Sense	40
Family Portrait with Father's Garden Awards	41
A Map Back Home	43
Homestead	44

III.

The Most Melancholic Key	48
Summer Solstice	50
Holding	51
Wild Flower or Faded Wreath	52
Mother Tended with Disembodied Hands	53
Poem for the Fourth Child	54
Yield	55
Common Goods	56
After the Prescribed Fire	57
Trappings	58
Bare	59
As the Apple Passes to Lilac	60

Hinge	61
For the Young Woman, a House	62
It Is the Ninth Day of Summer	63

IV.

The Harvest	66
A Poem for My Father on Snakes	67
A Poem for My Father on Flies	68
A Poem for My Father on Dogs	69
Evening Service	70
Dry	71
Father	73
A Poem for My Father on Raccoons	74
Father Sings for Supper and Severance	76
A Poem Absent of Animals for My Father	77
Father and Daughter, at the Adults with Dementia Home, Sit for Breakfast of Fried Eggs and Heirloom Tomatoes, Which Will Be Inherited	78
The Speed of Light Does Not Follow Any Acceptable Form of Logic	79
The Threshing Floor	80
Notes	85
Acknowledgments	88

Gratitudes 91

About the Author 93

I.

I Write You with the Intention of Amendment

Because you were a quart-berry basket filled with silver bells,
and I was the dried carrion carried by crows.
Because you were a fig tree with new roots,

and I, a garden of snakes. Because you were
a purse of gold coins, the last land of lands—
I have palmed this prayer in my pocket

till it turned to stone, and you housed this stone
in your heart until it turned to hardwood.
I have orphaned myself from the word

mother: the oxeye daisies pass to stiff asters as the bees
jump rabbit-foot clover, cone to cone, stitching the season
late is how I finished the family sampler

to cover the next generation's hope chest.
I need to scavenge the mother-daughter sentiment
from years of burnt eggs and runny oat, for I am done

arguing over tongues and the scorn of steel wool.
Matriarch, of the vine which scurries with myths
unseen, we have nursed through hunger's red music.

I create anew, name from your metronym and now understand—
momma, I write you with the intention of amendment, with thrift
to thrive penances: green as forgiveness, trepid as love.

There is a Third Eye to Every Memory: Part I

The sunlight broken by blinds
tells me I can tell you:
I lose things
a lot, I get dressed
three times before I leave the house
gate, tree, a sidewalk
with perfect cement squares
no weeds no ice heaving
to crack the seams
wait

the neighbor's cat on the porch says:
there are only one and two
bedroom apartments for rent
either in the basement or first floor
second if you lie about
the child

    I don't exist
endured as an adult
just now in my kitchen
dirty dishes and what I wanted
was not to lose my mother
or the heavy smell of summer
mosquitoes in your trap

the doctor said mother needed to kill me
and she made me otherwise
    died I have

the approaching night
reflected in the upper barn window
and I can tell you: things:
a dream dictionary, oil
a doll in the likeness of the devil
Barbie forks and spoons
cigarette smoke
a genetic code

the apiaries
tell me I can tell you:
I have no appetite
that I lost, young, my sense
of vocabulary a mute weight
inside an asylum of flesh

until she gives the voice
back I reverberate bees

Four Fields

Every winter, home
to the farm taken by marsh
thistle and wineberry. At the silo door,
the family eidolon absolves me
my stalk paper and indelible ink. A lifeline
borne from the tureen of their eyes—
cold soup, skinned.

.

My sister is always a rabbit.
My other, a grizzly.
I am a black swan, nested.

Survival is the dream
of a cicada midair,
a mass for the lost moon.

.

Here is the first of forty days:
the crop rent by runnels and sidereal
time. Mother, in early spring for her spade
riven by rocks, is found
clay-clad and weeping—
    What is *blood among blood?*
    What are *locusts from the hands of God?*

.

In his Sunday suit, the oldest
son remains plot-side.
My brother.
He is music not of the hand.
He is our father's headstone and glass decanter,
raised to the ergot sheaves.
Rose to the lip of the wind.

The Mother, Bird

      Blind! She opens her dream eye:
wild lilies and pinions unfurl as she lays
herself out in the long grass: a goose,
downy done, blue Bremen orbs, myopic

and dim. My body is a different bird.
It prefers the pine crown from the pen
though I peck *mama* until my beak breaks.
In her fledge-less field, I fowl the not being

wanted with the draw to dive from bough
and nest with her. If these sounding words
wrought action, I would turn feathers
for flesh, then kiss: be kissed.

I would turn typhlosis to sight, then see:
be seen, but look! She's no broody game.
O Mother bird, how was it beyond your ken
that Embdens are billed to be excellent parents.

There is a Third Eye to Every Memory: Part II

the clothesline says:
don't blink a different world
will exist or a different eye
will open a different lid

    if I stare long at a mirror:
    birds flinch into flight

    if I stare long at the sun:
    a white worm
    crawls out

the apple
tells me I can tell you:
there was a nun
she understood voodoo
could read tarot
knew the colors worn
by Santeria gods
knew novenas
could make me a saint

I will tell you:
as a child, I practiced stigmata
in the apartment's bathroom
but: no blood no nimbus
only fluorescent I
was lost rediscovered in
pallid skin and a dead language
myths I worship
and horde

I have seen Christ twice
once in the fifth grade he was:
tall, sandal-footed, robed, and glowing
he had no head
only a large revolving coin
walking Old Mammoth Road
he was coming for me

I lived on the second floor
a lie

White Grandfather Feathers and Inner Secondary Bone

If you watch, still, long enough, the birds will lift
a wing to expose the gift of their young.

      My mother had a murderous gaze. She hungered
like a garden unattended. Once, I came too near

the farmyard block: her strike posed midair
then one slick hand upon mine, clubbing

all over axe handle. Her upstroke stretched me out—
the hiss-thump sent serpents through the grass.

Blood bloomed, a small patch of bone, spillage,
then angels—the summer sun slamming

fresh against whitewash:

There is a Third Eye to Every Memory: Part III

the second time was in college
driving on the highway he hung
in a police turnaround
old leather, thorns, hair matted
caught in my high-beams
he raised his head—
          blood to blood and kin is kin
          (not once a phone call)

the psychiatrist
tells me to tell nothing: but
didn't you know I was
lost? didn't she know I was
ghost? that I needed
spectacular from my infancy
no knives no police no mother
atop my father no blood no—

the gold cross at steeple's top
tells: I need and still need:
wings
blisters on my feet
hallowed palms
a spear in my side
a prayer

in any tongue

In the Deep, Deep Woods on a Dark, Dark Night

The weight of stratification was pure;
older boys and I with want.
They would smile, then cuff the back of my head.

I would smile, then hold excitement still.
Truth being: I loved river grass
with its glume-like awns and culms.

But thirst came quick when south.
I couldn't scale the rock wall—
tennis-shoe soles too wet; the skin

on my knees tore the penned beginning.
I smelt the blood—*fee fi fo fum*:
he was taller than the rest, gangly, and pickerel ugly.

I cannot write what was lost near the black lake,
what swords. All I know is he turned
and woke to love's first kiss. When done, he lifted me

above moss and fern, button eyes, carried me home
past the other boys; bandaged both knees.
Happily ever, I schooled in silence then forgetfulness.

At recess, I would catch him catch me
at play like a child. He would stare.
I would stare. After. Once upon a time,

I was the milk girl; he the milk boy.
In the cafeteria, we would happen upon each other,
hands over the same blue and white

half-pint. In the beginning, I was wonder and Eros
had long arms, which wrapped around me
two-fold. Now, I am water reed. Now, I unbutton

my alphabet: all i's and o's.

Noun : Adjective : Idiom : Verb

It's the sound of ice from a tumbler: small
and round, but sure of how to care for itself—

It is a river of ink soft-seeping into the page.

It arrives in early morning: breaks
night down to shards of history—

It floats like a corpse: bobbing up, bobbing up.

It's a slim paper-cut kiss upon fingertip.
A stone passed from tongue to tongue—

It is held in the left hand as the right takes fire.

Today: Kinetic

Today: kinetic, rage-full, and head-ached; its throes immolate—

even as the towhee rustles backward, raking-up seeds
in the lynwood's leaf-litter; even as the morning-sun

lights the post and beam; the white barn,
outfield; the hen house, still—whose eggs

sizzle: in the metal skillet, on the metal burner, burn—

Next to the Child's Bed, a Gessoed Statue of Some Saint

The child knows she was there,
her life with no specifics. She
remembers a brass doorknob,
its capitulum shining, her hand out
of perspective: it might have been.

She remembers a farm, before the apartment,
cold and bare, with wheat hulls whirling.

She remembers some wood-covered wells,
which would collapse and vanish at random
into earthy holes, wormy roots, the copper
stench, and then the skulls. Always
the skulls: bird, ram, horse, human.

The child alone except for these ossein
dreams, her remembered bones.

.

The abstract oil hangs above the therapist's head as a nimbus.
What do you see in the painting today?

The child sees the Earth rotating and she feels the worms rotate in her.
She sees a metal whisk and feels all batter and warm vanilla.

The child sees a holy curve; she feels ashamed for Christ.

She sees a strand of hair and feels mapped out;
The child feels like a book with all the answers.

She sees the crest of a skull, feels: there is the key.

.

The child loves:

that pencil smell, pancakes, vampires, blood, being alone, frankincense and
myrrh, fog, goats, encyclopedias, confined spaces, cupcakes, bells, the ocean, egg

nog, tarot decks, the color red, oboe music, fur coats, angel food cake, quilts, baby Jesus, rubies, darkness.

.

The child fears:

corpses, chicken meat, centipedes, drowning, darkness, water, blood, zombies, the color blue, spiders, God, being alone, wooded areas, cutlery, bath tubs, balloons, rain, public restrooms, open graves, frogs, Hell, Heaven, the Devil, loud noises, corn fields, bees.

.

Next to the child's bed, a gessoed statue of some saint.

.

She remembers her prayers.

> The instruments used: a placemat, a knife, raw chicken meat, a nurse's uniform.

Now I lay me down to sleep.
> Next instruments used: the closet, ice cream, a rain coat, blood, a spoon.

I pray the Lord my soul to keep.
> Remaining instruments used: runny oatmeal, the bathroom sink, feces, a tube of red lipstick.

If I should die before I wake,

the child remembers,
> *I pray the Lord my soul to take.*

.

The child had a toy chest at the base of her bed.
She would empty it, climb in, and close the lid:
a satin pillow, pall, wood lacquer, and the child

with two, skeletal fingers raised in blessing and latch.

II.

Statue

I stare at your likeness:

one hand raised in blessing,
the other exposing

a lucent heart, flame, and thorn.
From kneeling, I rise

and touch your feet. Press
my head against coarse paint.

I believe you are more than gesso.
I believe you are more than

a cross and swaddling.
Here, a long inhale. (*I believe*

I will burn within you).
A bell tolls and breath

unsettles the dust.

Scene with Apparitions

I'll-Cut-Your-Goddamned-Eyes-Out empties her tumbler to muddle at your hip, softly arcing her olive branches, but do not fall for this thigh trick, continue to Pull-Out-Your-Chest-Hairs, one by one, with your forefinger and thumb, filling the sink's metal yawn with wires and cross wires until the shock of it all wakes The-Go-Between-Child, who runs their tin cup across cabinets, rattles the plates and mugs from their shelves—ceramics scatter on the floor as carpals, metacarpals, phalanges: you remember a time—when the spirit of who your mother was, but is not now, lifted you in her arms and pointed to the door, said, *See this, this is my blood, and this, and this*, now under the halogen round the knives break into blade song for they love this story with all their teeth. They riot their block, want you bare-chested and blind, but you are done with ghosts. You walk right out, leaving bleached flour on the threshold and an anklet of crimson cord tied in nines around iron bells for this sinner's scene, this sweet recollection that cuts a conscience clean.

Triptych Depicting an Average Morning, Miracles, and the Corpse

It's 11 a.m., a Friday, in boardinghouse bed
I wake to the electronic ringtone of a cell:
    and I am in love with poetry::
    how the body remembers its carbon:
    Christmas in the right hand: 1st kiss about the neck:
        the corpse by my eyes:

I do not turn it off until standing
to avoid backsliding into sleep, yet I
refuse glasses::

I strip to the flesh:
    astounded by my memorylove
    of rot: blue, black, brown, purple, greygreen:: I adore
    the beauty found in wounds:
        the art of decomposition:

don robe, grab key card: lumber to the bathroom:: remember
        my sister used to check behind the shower curtain every trip:

shampoo, conditioner, shave under arms, then legs:
    the body as individualized jazz instruments:
lather jasmine soap:
    tenor sax, bass, and drum, the piano
        for a recently deceased man::

I drip back to door # 9:
    striving toward a musical whole

slide ID: punch the access code by rote touch:
top middle, then top right, bottom left, end with top right
enter woodblock room:
    a utilitarian aesthetic: like the break
    of an Atlantic wave upon New England rocks:
        my sister knew him, too, but only fresh after bath::

I dry my legs:
    now: violaceous, under fluorescent lights:
    his ligaments rigored, limbs akimbo::

    according to weather.com: currently 56°, feels like 56°, cloudy::
        I believe in the religion of a cherry blossom,
        the taste of saki, plum wine:

            his skin cratered from rotbloat,
            torso hollowed to an open mouth:
10% chance of precipitation, high of 78°::
        warm unagi in oyster sauce,
a capri and sweater day::
        my clouds resemble fish
        saba sashimi, tako: complete with cups:

praise socks: cotton with arch support::
            rib bones as yellowed teeth, hardened fatclump gums,
            desiccated viscera, sex dried to a knotted shell::
        I don't even know who he is.

        Then a child, I asked: *Why won't the man get up?*
    Why am I allergic to bee venom,
susceptible to the contagion of yawns?
        My sister answered: *Family:: means not asking questions.*

                :: means shotgun forgetting: means no, no
                recollection: means skinsuit walking: means::

no blisters today.
    I am confounded by the color orange::
        dumbfounded how this body is our body.

In Fief or Fee

You have ceded the Lord of your youth.
Your sight leaves the body. The Sight
not to return to your body as tenant,
as mud and spit and miracles, or was it
apostasy that jilted you? A blind save
off to a river. You cannot witness
allegiance in myth or in science, yet we
conceived across history. A vision stemmed
from cells, petri or embryonic: born.
Is it fealty sent or fealty seen?
We are a country—
with or without a flag.

Out of Eden, From the Amtrak Window

all-hollow-boned beasts,
with no bladders, fly

tiny birds, evolutionary
exemplars, the count thus far:

a woodpecker, three cardinals, one indigo
bunting in the air, an early morning

dove, but truly, a vulture.
There is already too much waste—

a train kid hustling a dollar, no really, four
abandoned mattresses where compounds

crust. It took going all the way
from Arcadia before the first, rusted

hull, a slight slant to my head, but I swore
there was something of a starred flag.

Right now, the woman next to me
has entered a foreign country.

Her hands as pressed pages turn
a dry leafy sound between us

snakes, a tag and a skin, hung
on the walls, painted a dozen times

over. There is food tied in bags
to the trees, near the bridges.

There is a sign that reads: *see,
these are the signs.*

Mirror, Mirror

There is no tree of knowledge. No
animals named in thy glory.

Jezebel, there is only 20/20 sweat
in this community of weeds. Only pathos,
salt, and God's trick—
                silent as bread is
the unease in your belly, crab
crawling like a disciple. I have
felt it too. Black lines around our eyes.

To trump this telamon myth,
Jezebel, create a new fear
with words, hem up womanhood.

Appoint yourself by namesake only,
gather in the stench of blood—
planked pocket, rust cradle
sticky pine enamel with nickel nails.

I will put your suffering in order:
horns and tooth, blood and cock feathers.

There is beauty, Jezebel—
desire that slows the breath,
a mirage in the heat of eyes,
half-slit vision of corpses.
The plowboys are asleep,

all stark moonbeams
in brown house graves.
We are the mint land.

I know you want a love affair,
a bit of truth, a bowl of nuts,
tear-shaped meat fitting your tongue.
We exist by skin on skin,
darkening redemption, a ribbon
tied around the wrist.

Blood can live again in you, bone bare:
first in dreams then hands
then in fists then mysteries.

You will learn to float while alive or afterwards.

Jezebel, you are a house united.
Naming the demons binds them back to shadow.
                         Yes, I grapple with God.

Jezebel, do you
remember that ill-tempered saint?
How at every red light at every

street corner—he'd stop and call our name?
A filigree dance, mid-air
birds at the hearth—

There is no metaphor to carry this fire.

Attending

Again, the wind burns up the barn side
and snow flames off the roof.

Our men have gone uphill,
all leather gloves, knifes, and boiling

water borne from the well
to wrought-iron warming on the wood.

Inside, women coil in coats.
We stand, our bodies touch. We eat

blood oranges until our tongues swell.
In the morning, all animal stalls

are empty—because of love, we hide
rinds like hunger in our gardens. Wait—

by gates to receive the halos of mist lifting from pines.

Self Portrait with Hand Study and Jung's Word Association Test

There you superannuate (as in antiquated, as prove
obsolete) an excessive prefix, a fifth meta-

carpal (as in situated behind or beyond [as in
grandmother, mother, daughter, XX chromosome])

hamate bone all hammered up. Little pink
pinkie, what to do phalanx (as in osseous, in itchy

finger) with calcification (as in rigidity, as in
hardening by impregnation [as saturate, fill throughout])

conceive? The use for corset so different now
since youth (as in rogue, as in *wee wee wee*—)

wanton, the green (as in not properly aged)
arrogance (as in an offensive display) of a high

school pep or a dry hump until chapped
in the back library stacks, such fine paper

tiger lines (as an appearance of strength) this hand
(as properly middle-aged [as insignificant])

has written—*all the way home*. Reams
of Times New Roman, font 12, format set to

No Spacing (as in memories running red
rover: as in marksman, as in bullet [holed])

O grave New England sky (as in granite face [stiff lip])
O arthritic ache (as in afflicted) upon pen and

sticky trigger: this ode of black bile and measure
owed to lousy melancholy, barometric pressure.

If Your Family Owned a Mausoleum, then This Poem Would Make More Sense

Your sisters have found corpses: beautiful
one in the bath, the other hell
bent on their driving wheel, you say
your corpse has not yet been
behind cabinet door, scythed between
the smooth S-folds of faucet pipes under
sink nor face down, undercurrent, bumping bloated
limbs underbrush in bog water.

    Your body has been undertaking the weight
of preposition and place, you say, so easily
you'd swear it was still alive: laid bare
against the far corner's molding
under bed, underage, you, un-
derfoot-tow-tone-cut-press-pin
but you don't dare mind, you know
you'll find it *close to home*—

like your second brother bid, *it will be*
considered self-afflicted, understated,
and no one speaks of the elder, underroof
under God's thumb, your dead's
stuporous shuffle to their plots. Stories
hidden in plain sight, you say, ghosts
and coroners, triggers set
the tongue to toll, yet underkill.

Family Portrait with Father's Garden Awards

My Dear Middle Flower,

Your bracts have curlicued
the catkin quivered; night did linger—
a blowzy-noser with familiar tropes and plot lines.

Yes, m'greenspice, beneath this canopy, relations do
alarm so easily, make no bouquet about it
or the sheer reason home smells of peat.

        What strange possession in you now,
my taciturn Irish twin, to tongue
slip our code cached in cant and bloviation.

Shhhh… our family endogamy keeps blooming
claim no resemblance, no resemblance
both of us not wanting that pedestrian kiss

or these anemochorous memories
hidden in hermetic highness and archaic diction,
yet I'll front a little farce-face girl

to stave the truth terror of being found
out it comes, down to this
deflected neurosis: reflected sorosis

sister, I need you: one Molly bush
to one Molly bloom whisper weed and spread
through this, our floricultured bed—Go!

     sing the hard work of what's not been
… O silence for silence sake, pray us
from the kitchen vase. I know we must

cross ourselves, a blackbird hybrid,
join against the one swaggering head
over the dying the newly cut—

                blank: don't I dare! mistake
water doused as clichéd drowned
father's pruners as right as rain

—as right as rain on coralbells; please, for
a god's well-being: don't tell, and do
do tell on us two—

Love,
Your Coralbell

A Map Back Home

A girl drifts along the corridors of her body and wonders
if she remembers how to open her right atrium.
With blood, there is always something at the threshold:
a lung, an eye, a breast-bone suffocating, but what
of second-cut grain or the braided fingers
of strawberry vines—the girl recalls the clay
lamp she sculpted in Sunday school,
how the burning was symbolic for something lost
from patchwork quilt to basement to root cellar—
the small, dank pit—a womb: her map begins

here. A woman turns new lamps from tuber skins,
hangs one at each lymph node, vessel valve. She
illuminates every statue of Christ, every winter home.
To be in the map and of the map: She
moves by visceral touch and infrared heat;
yet nights when the wind bleats and the axe
contacts the block, she bears between
seraphim and brimstone, myth and the family
tree: ingrained, but still the woman's chapter and verse.
Her own heart now to pitter-patter, knell, lie or limn.

Homestead

The wind tugs the sweet gale; the pepperbush bobs in the thicket.

Ice thaws in the brook out back—
    mud-fossil footprints where the child ran,
    learnt the ways of serpent and bee.

    These were my fields.

March-bog where I nursed the lack
of barn swallows nested in rafters, away—

Why does winter return me?
To old, gray snow; white paint, ill and peeling—

    They have remodeled the front barn and the silo, clean gone.

Sentimentality—my small enchanter's
nightshade, you cliff seep my bones; leave me—
    these were My fields.

The jolt-April breeze disturbs; there should be no fear in this plot.

    I am no longer that wild buttonbush.

III.

The Most Melancholic Key

My lineage knows how to load a gun,
knows how to work the screw and vise,

how to trim the fat and wield the knife.
I'd like to talk about my mother in current light

the pounding piano chords, which cut to strings
in Balmorhea's *The Winter*, yet she died in fall

a fall, then fall, and I don't know
if it's cello or violin. I would have once

had faith, and I don't
know what will come of the pudding

or out in the wash. I need no tears, only the blood
serum levels, the toxicology report.

I want every pill counted, every cell, each biochemical
compound, five-carbon sugar ring accounted, proof: *why*

did you have to die?—what a ridiculous line
like her cellular clock was to continue its metronome

regardless of springs or the laws of energy.
To persist, that's what mothers and myths do—

leave no whetting stone, stick to guns, yet question
theories, retest, repeat, refute the shortening days,

the telomere's nucleotide sequence on DNA strands,
rendered tallow with wicks too lost to ignite.

This must be violin for it has whipped
to a wail. Things my mother loved

and let go: brass bells, pewter plates and bowls,
owl feathers, all her fire opals.

The cardiologist gave a clean bill of health;
mother was spent with cleanliness and clichés.

Time she was done with, her aging, self-ended
coda, my doubt, strung in C sharp minor / D flat.

Summer Solstice

Mother, it would be your birthday in thirteen days,
a baker's cliché followed in weeks by the crepe
myrtle's explosion of father's own fading.

    Today I am assessing the parts of the sum—
I have noticed my own weakened epiglottis, the chronic
throat clearing, the increase in choking on fluid

and foods, words thick as silence.
How does one learn to speak again? Mother, my tongue
furrowed and coated, couched against the hard

palate, since your quiver and fib—atrial and pace
cleared, clotting coagulation cleared, your hands
crossing yourself. Even in sleep, you're still a myth

maker. I am questioning all the time.
Could my childhood asthma have been
a congenital heart anomaly? The elevated

liver enzymes, your old drink? Fat deposited
deep within fetal lobules, an inheritance
from father's orphaned genome, who

knows, but the clock's dry watch
a prebought plot for a life
stilled, every June.

Holding

One moment, the farmland is covered with old snow,
the next, fog-shrouded and clayed-underfoot.

I turn the field, afraid of the flux in temperature
having to lose again my heady till to verglas,

but the croft thaws as with her first homecoming:
the seeded contraction, the body's breath

priming pump, the womb's door. —My plot
clear, the maiden returns, and only the seasoned

stone wall retains its rime while a single crocus shoot
silently rises, and the cedar waxwing cries: *See! See!*

Wild Flower or Faded Wreath

The morning clouds in valley, still
rain over the mountain peaks.
A dead fox roadside and crows gather

home, like my dead: clung to me as
this wet wool, damp from garden run.
This has happened before; on the hall

table: the flower vase, new again—
which holds whatever is placed within
it with equal, tender balance.

Yet I cannot help but see womb;
see mother: cream and bottom heavy, berthed
in place, at the stations of the house:

stove, sink, washroom, judge of content
and by content. Mother: standing with arms
outstretched, our sheets on the linen line

bleached, sun-fresh and winding.

Mother Tended with Disembodied Hands

her forearms deep in the wash basin, ruddy
knuckles livered by labor, then lopped
off and oft by water's sharp edge.
On days when drought wizened the well,

mother would arm herself with dowsing rods.
When fever struck the farm, mother would crest
a wreath of pasture berry. When rot ripened the silo
mother would quarry stone for the marker, plot

wood lilies for witness; August
heat billows cumuli to cumulonimbus, and I
lay corded to this gestational bed, recognition
long as the life-lined palm. We are the same

one in royalty, rabble, the immolator, and
then the immolation. Mother,
though your hands have gone to torch,
I still bring matches to your temple daily.

Our schizophrenic heat, I can intern
combust: nine-month lava effusive, pyroclastic in me,
and I without a dry chemical extinguisher.
I carry a pyre of illness, so easily

passed to child: her fennel fingers, novas—
every polydactyl digit conceived a burnt wick.
My constitution's gentry has called me to court
charged with arson and use of smoke signals

Puff: the brown bat fattens in flight
Puff: the barred owl hoots from her branch
Puff: am I risking too much? Genetics remain
as the night rain's bartered relief splatters through

window, tamps heredity's tinderbox sensible.
My unborn child's hands, unfamiliar
yet to fire; my own hands weighted with soot; and
mother's unfleshly folding, and unfolding, in water, and not.

Poem for the Fourth Child

There are many things to consider:
wondrous billow of kitchen curtain,
the blackbirds as they school the sky
against a cloud, the waxwing's bittersweet
tips, or the cells we carry—our medical
imaging. What to do when chromosomes,
spindled apart, nettle instead of pair?
Our mother and father: perspiration pinned.
Their chest cavities all blood quake and grasp
for care. Such perfume went into you—
four legs, four arms, lungs, sinew—prayer.
For cynosure you are a God, and what it is
of God: resin and stardust, covered mirror
a pressed shirt. You are cleaned, then clothed as just
the other day: after the caul and secudines,
after the baptismal, you! Alive
with responsiveness for and before
our eyes, your hands upraised
white flags to the glory, bane in the air.

Yield

In the river, sledges of ice
          off the dried banks. The last
corn has been cut; the field, felled.
          These are harvest givens:
stubble will rot and go to post;
          rime will thicken on beds,
culled crop; now not, my house—
          a photo box of stills;
hidden in pantry, preserve jars
          aborted; minutes embalmed in hours.
What grows the length of a nail
          harrows the rooted vetch. My season
corollary: sod, a coulter
          blade, six pome seeds. Should not
a mother search for her lost
          share; would not the scion
     surrender?

Common Goods

      and in my dream, your mother
has bought us a mask and mantle

kitten who embodies every unconditional
criterion.

I pin and play her belly
to my skin. Her kitten teeth scrape

a sting.
          A conception, so

desired that I feel it even now, here—
in pith, where a pelage laid.

I go to the bank, then the market.
Buy shallots and eggs.

Buy seedless grapes.

After the Prescribed Fire

It has been a long time: this field
reclaimed by cedar saplings, bone

roots cross under earthworks once singed,
savanna-like pines still stand, heat

hollowed, whose perches couch a tawny plume
—lone hawk's cypher eyes do rove

talon tally down to woodland vole.
      Here is the morning wake: this sunrise

successional, stage of red, a sash
athwart an ember breast, withered

wreath with ribbons tressed, now littered
days, lorn, and rust, in truss my heart

with grief, the simple loss of us.

Trappings

The night sky passes to a paler shade.
The lake ice has gone out, dredging

the morning fog through the patch garden.
At the east window, what have I built?

Bone cradle, stolen blood, what shelter
with occupants, miniature and contained:

Lionels without track;
a doll with one eye; time-dried

boxes of rookies, reeds, and lace;
glass shooters. The rafters are full

of ghosts: the bassinet in the far corner
is seen, even now, lambent, through

the mote haze: wooly bear, fresh buntings
the flesh, buttercream. Now the sky

has reached its high blue; at windowpane,
no plant yields fruit. I have dressed

again, this wooden berth. I swear
to you, I live alone.

Bare

I have neglected my canning
for a full season spent in search
of a maid wreathed by wild

spicewood, alive and showy,
yet just: this hulled sunflower
where dark-eyed juncos mob

millet and cracked corn
among the pine brush. A thaw
and depressions pock

nests of grasses, moss to couch
clutches of brown blotched eggs; soon
winter bird, two weeks less a day,

your young will leave upon fledging
while the last snow falls across field
and the farm cat hastens its hunt—

I have no words for lack that holds
late into a mother's spring
harder than the blue ice.

As the Apple Passes to Lilac

the flickers' *kee* coalesces with the late rains—
mid-May damp wood: the field fence needs mending;
but the tender has not yet roused, though I have watched
all morning, the eastern towhee build her nest.
I am house done—my fall bird roosted, no room
for nestlings. This frame: no braided branch.
The towhee's mate returns to post: *drink your tea,*
—drink your tea

Hinge

In the room upstairs
a sturdy bed: marrow soft, filled
with the bodied smell of honeyed milk.

To be mother, must mean to be wax
solidified over yield; to be the rubber
ring in Ball jar; the hinge on pantry door;

hymen then womb then symphysis.
The bearing says: open 90 degrees, let go 45.
Every morning, I wait for the bound

downstairs, the child's bid: toast with jam;
my desired movement for these two, set axes
occurs so fiercely in me, I fear: what now?

A return to carpenter, bee,
garden: my bed has been abandoned
for years, the bread consumed;

and as for my bony doorknocker—
that, too, shall decay: neither
fossil nor fruit preserved.

For the Young Woman, a House

You are at school. I return home.
Our atoms, superposition. Physicists say
the cat is both living and dead in equal parts.
Lest the cat be a bird, the bird
a young woman, the woman a house to an abstract
like trust. Here, but then not; but then—
haven't we all been that spirit?
At the window, a chickadee alive with chirps.
I exist in a state of return
to pane and sill, it's plain still—not
even a downy tuft. This is the way:
I will go to work as the bird.
You will eat lunch at noon like the cat.
Our atoms will be here, we trust

It Is the Ninth Day of Summer

rain with humidity, high as the turkey tail
laddering-up the hardwood.

There are crepuscular rays: a quick dart
of goldfinch, the yellow inch
worm scaling the fibrous stalk

of tansy, while green June bugs
buzz iridescent infinity-loops
above the deer tongue grass, cicadas

change rhythm in the tulip trees
when the wet breeze lifts leaves to flash
silver blades; all day you mistook

strangers' faces for someone you knew—
that joyous current, buoyant, then the abrupt
recognition of your mistake, the fact

of the matter being: the person
you love and miss is still dead.

IV.

The Harvest

The leaves are down. March
mud slick from frost, this

morning, my breath is
the scratch of limbs.

Ahead, from apple crate or child's
palm,

small piece of purple
tissue paper

wraps the last bole.
Lent is a season

of final thoughts, fruitless
with the loss of you.

By our faith in apples,
what could save us?

And beyond all this,
a mound of dirt,

splintered wood
for a barrow.

A Poem for My Father on Snakes

Just now, a sudden tang of smoke
    though no one in this house

has burned in a while. I am
    having a hard time

this morn suited in its best ash,
    its length mastered that of the long boards

—your shadow,
    getting done the things it needs to get done.

I think the sound of scales
    passing through the underbrush

fathers a different voice than the passing
    of a paw—

the spirit around the cold blood
    has a heft heavier

than air weighted with my own
    associations: like something before

ancient, someone outside of the right hand
    like a breathtaking hymn cast out.

A Poem for My Father on Flies

Flies are not interested in islands
of memory stored as microscopic chemical
changes. Flies do not care

about one's synaptic plasticity or the notches
in metal tags about your neck,
whether for placement in mint or tooth

gap. One government fact, one lively story
like Santa Claus or our fly-boys
over-the-pole cold, war: yours—

something at LADD air field, operation White
Alice; something about turboprops, Dye 3, and flying
boxcars; ice caps and wave flutter—search

radars with dual antenna; all your memories tropospheric
scatter, lost to back EMFs, geopathic stress,
secrets from Greenland and the AK

DEW line, coded in tongues and of tongues
torn out. One government conspiracy, one living
fact. Flies do not adhere to man-drawn borders on a map

and as such may be found beyond their (en)listed reach.
Tonight, there is more than diptera circling through the sky.

A Poem for My Father on Dogs

There are dogs in this poem.
They eat chicken bones and foil

wrappers. There are crows, a whole
robed and murderous slew.

This is supposed to mean something,
this verse where you pull an ace

comb from your pocket.
Its teeth turn to teeth,

break from their shaft.
I watch your face for expression.

Any *rat-a-tat-tat* gunfire flight,
any bullet shell bounce-up,

yet only your crooked grin, enamel
rain of incisors and crowns

how the noise startles like that
of a western jacquard, its snaps ripped

                            open
this is what time does to us.

Evening Service

Look, how odd the street
light through stained glass.
The fading crepuscule of ecru
edging toward a bruised brown
and here, the dark oil
patina of the Good Samaritan.
Follow it down to the illuminated wound,
burgundy and rum give way to
pallor, and those hills where,
past the mosaic, a well rises from broken stone.
Across its topmost lip, worn
grooves from rope burn and palm.
Here she waits for him.
Hair pulled back, tie in
a blade of grass. Her collation
of fruit long forgotten in folds.
Her fragile face turned toward the road, for
all things circle to water, and
she believes he will come
out of the amber glass, the cold
lead breakers.

Dry

The screwdriver, loose in the hand,
tightens the hen house door and dismisses
the cat who sleeps hard-boiled. At sunrise,
images of Jesus: yellow-eyed and milky
through the morning fog, the hens to trough
leave behind their eggs. I cannot steal
this lot, but O' the bee's honey—heavy

enough to be suspect; Jesus as Molotov
cocktail created specifically to burn
smoke-stunned: the honey-comb guilts apart.
Tonight, there will be star-stains and gravity
folding the white pines in upon themselves
as in grace, as in Tanqueray and Sue Bee;
Jesus as shopping bag caught in the canopy.

Ponder this: inside every quinary bundle
inside every plastic polymer, a body
singing before it enters the flesh (right now
a cell has mutated [my tongue]). Jesus, there is
wind through the window linen now and again
now, a voice: condensation caught between
two panes, storm and inner—the bullet shell

frost-heaved from winter marsh, thaw-found.
Pardon this: the sulfur smell, the deafening
exit; how we broke with spade the night
ice, all six feet of it—and no one spoke
a word, the hive mummed. At dawn the birdsong
drowned out the bells as we picked dead
bee casings from each other's palms.

Jesus, this is all I can safely canary—our history,
bones sung silent, relics we bear to bear.
The cat, called confession, now awake and walking
out: past the pines & hemlocks, the penny-royal
the rusty-nail, loosey-goose, the wire
& the reed, brittle-bobbing, in the wind. Witness:
"No one will ever know!" Jesus as silencer, hush-

blood and yo ho ho. The chicken coop, tight
with cackleberries left to crack into chorale
the family hymnal. I have juiced, all: the 45,
the apiary, the bee-keeper, the wild turkey;
virgins troth *dry* in the tabernacle.

Father

It began: curbstone. gutter.
a foot. followed through. a natural
swing to the arms. and then

narrowing streets. the hill: steep.
now steeper. until blue
broke from your brow.

your hand rising to ribs. late
summer rustling. this small breeze. a
stranger passing too close. and you say:

I have to stop.

.

I am a house of your house—
salt, bone, even this thick skin love
of words I have written: *you*
again, in single subject
notebooks, bound with wire,
your chest

an open lotus
casement
miter box
chevron
one straining beam
the spathe of
a calla lily.

A Poem for My Father on Raccoons

For the past three days, I have watched the raccoon
bloat from the sun on the side of the road.
Its fur, a matted ferrous brown, has formed

into spires, which are slowly lifting skyward.
Arched by the taut skin beneath, like an arrow
fletched to a shaft, and then pulled

up to an archer's shoulder, keen eye,
a constellation of potential energy,
not wasted like these kinetic crows

who swoop low and lower still, but we
are not to speak of corvids circling in poems,
or their carrion, but what of that we carry?

What you are doing in your own house—
Papa: a word I never called you.
Stacking your boxes of other families' photos

gathered from the dump's *still good* shed
or torn from magazines. On Monday you move
the boxes against the opposite wall; on Tuesday

you move them back; on Wednesday you move the boxes
against the opposite wall—such commotion. How you *went
to school with all of them*, and the dust

of disease settles on your record
player, your oak furniture, your colorful
ceramics like the painted egg with gold clasp

you gave your granddaughter, who carried
and cared for it as Faberge. How she drew
a smiley face in red marker

on the cotton boll we picked last vacation.
She named the tuft Fred, and it lived in the egg
for years, but there's no need for this frivolity,

or birds and how they flock, or myths
because all this is fancy for how your blood
seeped across plasma membranes, every cell drowned

down to dementia. A diffusion you could not control,
memories overwritten or replaced, your boxes
remain—one broken link in your amino

acid chain, one poorly folded protein, un-
chaperoned. These are the facts, Papa.
I do believe in belomancy, our feathered lots

tossed to ether, their trajectory little known,
and I hope the DOT will pick up the raccoon
before rupture, as your cells, from all this heat.

Father Sings for Supper and Severance

What survives? My sister's ruth;
a deed composition; his subject-verb
disagreement, father's dementia
paling his eyes. The trust in our family

farm, marginalized. *We have less
rhodora and ground blueberry than
before.* Bind and yoke the oxen, rib-thin
—a second thought: everything is here.

We have always had chickens and beef.
Gut and liver, beloved throat
with aged esophagus, Eat! Take up
the tine, tune and sing, *to cattle, to cattle!*

I will wrestle long the withered heath.
—She will feed you: everything lese here.

A Poem Absent of Animals for My Father

I am waiting for my father / to return to the body of / my father, the man / that was in his body / looking like / my father, to return / to this body / his body / to return, the man / the man, my father looks like / rightly / to his body / I am waiting / for the body of my father to return / the who / the man, my father

was—all of this is
to say:

the body in the chair next to mine
and the man in the chair next to me
in the body

that is my father
and is not anything *of* my father
in this body, I grieve

he is still alive.

Father and Daughter, at the Adults with Dementia Home, Sit for Breakfast of Fried Eggs and Heirloom Tomatoes, Which Will Be Inherited

This morning, in not my house
what to do except clear away
not my dishes from a meal, not mine

wash in water—*such a wonder*
unfamiliar as this language spoken
not through my lips that I have

The Speed of Light Does Not Follow Any Acceptable Form of Logic

my father is outside the locked ward and my sister

both my sisters and my brother

our father keeps his coat on at all times

my father is in a world where I am his mother
my husband is the man from the laundromat
my brother-in-law is the man from the bank

the light we can see in tonight's sky is from stars already left

the light we can see and the coat

the nurses at the locked ward will quickly jump and run the length of their stations to sound the alarm

when my father left this world he stayed in this world

he will not be in this world again

everyone wants him to be locked in the ward with his coat except for him

our father is unhappy here

father wants to be folded into a neat tight triangle
of stars

the light we can see

it is tired
it has traveled a very long way
it wants to come in and remove its coat

The Threshing Floor

Goats were pouring forth their pure milk.
Anemones were piercing the road's ribs.
Lice were biting the seers gathered in gawk.
Almonds were blanching in bowls of cruor.
Teeth were breaking gum or falling out.
Breath was fouling close to necks, to ears.
Tongues were separating themselves.
Houses were massing their shadow's length.
Letters were uniting into lenten plots.
 Who do you believe me to be?
   Is not the same as
     Who do you say that I am?

A gravel path raked by death dragging
  is the same as a bloom
    on the staff of life.

.

Wheatgrass covers the field
where once switchblade and broom
sage grew, big and little
blue stem, wild rye—the word *preserve*
in Late Latin means *'to keep /
in advance of'* coming rows,
soft red winter, your brother:
an ancient grain, our ancestors,
roots not native to this soil.

.

The devil hath desired to sift us as wheat.
Tillers and mainstem cut down: sickle, then scythe
then reaper-binder, the wheat flail working
loose the berries, the wind awhistle through
the straw as the sparrow shrieks.

.

This land, before fallow field or cultivated crop,
before stolen and bloodshed, before we
forced our own history upon it, before
we faithfully answered, *Who do you believe me to be*,
before our weaknesses were revealed in the winnowing
and we falsely witnessed, *Who do you say that I am*,
let us relearn Latin, relearn, as in *conserve*
'to keep / together,' may the land take us to breast,
may the land carry us under her arm, as if
we were omers of wheat to sieve
and knead into a rough hewn boule—
      may the land leave us out to prove,
            may we rise, together, by grace.

Notes

"The Mother, Bird"
Lines 10 and 11 are a nod to Abigail Adams's quote, "…we have too many high sounding words and too few actions that correspond to them."

"In the Deep, Deep Woods on a Dark, Dark Night"
Many classic fairy tales and children's rhymes have been woven throughout the poem, but special attention is drawn to 'fe fi fo fum,' taken from the classic English fairy tale, "Jack and the Beanstalk," ca. 1890:
"Fee-fi-fo-fum,
I smell the blood of an Englishman,
Be he live, or be he dead
I'll grind his bones to make my bread."

"Next to the Child's Bed, a Gessoed Statue of Some Saint"
Contains a version of a child's bedtime prayer, ca. 18th century.

"In Fief or Fee"
Lines 2 through 6 are a very loose re-telling of the Biblical story, 'Pool of Siloam,' found in John 9: 7. Lines 8 and 9 are a nod to the use of stem cells to treat blindness.

"Mirror, Mirror"
Line 6 is not mine. I have researched and researched the phrase to find the original poet, but with no avail. I read the poem in my youth, and the line always stayed with me.

"Self Portrait with Hand Study and Jung's Word Association Test"
Lines 10 and 17 are taken from "This Little Piggy" by Mother Goose, ca. 1760.

"Family Portrait with Father's Garden Awards"
Line 10 is a jesting to part of Robert Pinsky's quote on Strunk and White's *The Elements of Style*, "…I fell in love with Strunk & White's loathing for cant and bloviation, the ruthless cutting of crap, jargon, and extra words…"

Lines 28 and 29 are a nod to Theodore Roethke's "Flower Dump."

"The Most Melancholic Key"
Balmorhea. "The Winter." *Rivers Arms*, composed by Robe Lowe and Michael A. Muller, Western Vinyl, 2012.

"Wild Flower or Faded Wreath"
Lines 8 and 9 are a direct quote from Jane Hirshfield, "Between the Material World and the World of Feeling," *After* (New York: Harper Perennial, 2006) 84.

"Mother Tended with Disembodied Hands"
Line 17 contains the archaic adjective 'intern' (also seen, 'interne') meaning "internal."

"Yield"
Lines 8 through 10 are a nod to the works of Eleni Sikelianos within *Body Clock*, Coffee House Press, 2008.

"Bare"
Impetus from the Demeter/Persephone Homeric Hymn, ca. 6th century, BC.

"For the Young Woman, a House"
Lines 2 and 3 are a nod to Schrodinger's cat, a thought experiment within quantum physics.

"A Poem for My Father on Flies"
Lines 10 and 11 mention operation "White Alice," which, in full, was the White Alice Communications System (WACS): a US Air Force communication system used during the Cold War. It consisted of around 80 radio stations with antennas running through Alaska. My father was an US Air Force Pilot that flew the DEW line, as well as a radio specialist helping build, run, and maintain WACS.

Lines 18 and 19 are a nod to a quote found online while researching flies, "…please understand that insects do not adhere to man-drawn borders on a map and as such they may be found beyond their listed 'reach' showcased on our website…" (http://www.insectidentification.org/insects-by-state.asp?thisState=Washington)

"Dry"
'Yo ho ho' has many shanty variations, this use nods to the quote from Robert Louis Stevenson within *Treasure Island*, "Fifteen men on the Dead Man's Chest Yo-ho-ho, and a bottle of rum! Drink and the devil had done for the rest Yo-ho-ho, and a bottle of rum!" ca. 1882.

"Father Sings for Supper and Severance"
Line 14 contains the archaic verb 'lese' meaning "to lose."

"The Speed of Light Does Not Follow Any Acceptable Form of Logic"
The title is a direct quote from HubPages by @quicksand, ca. 2011.
(http://quicksand.hubpages.com/hub/light--as-we-know-it)

The poem is mirrored off of Michael Dickman's section "VII" in his poem, "Stations," from *Flies*, Copper Canyon Press, 2011.

"The Threshing Floor"
This work was created for the *Writing the Land* Project, a collaboration between poets and protected lands; and was inspired by Malvern Hills Farm, an 871-acre property in Henrico County and Charles City County, Virginia, protected by *Virginia's Capital Region Land Conservancy*.

Lines 10 and 12, and then repeated further in the poem are variants of New Testament Scripture where Jesus questions his disciples.

The third section opens with a nod to the New Testament Scripture wherein the Devil has called for Simon Peter.

Acknowledgments

Grateful acknowledgment is made to the editors of the following journals, print and online, and anthologies, in which earlier versions of these poems, sometimes under different titles, first appeared:

The Antioch Review: "Homestead."
Ballard Street Poetry Journal: "A Map Back Home," "Father."
The Banyan Review: "It Is the Ninth Day of Summer," "Summer Solstice."
Berkeley Poetry Review: "Yield," "Trappings."
The Bitter Oleander: "Attending."
Dămfīno: "The Mother, Bird," "Common Goods."
Ethel: "Scene with Apparitions."
Hayden's Ferry Review: "The Most Melancholic Key."
Hinchas de Poesía: "Mirror, Mirror."
Hotel Amerika: "There's a Third Eye to Every Memory" (Parts I-III), "Statue," "Four Fields."
Hunger Mountain Review: "A Poem for My Father on Snakes," "A Poem for My Father on Flies," "A Poem for My Father on Dogs," "A Poem Absent of Animals for My Father," "The Speed of Light Does Not Follow Any Acceptable Form of Logic."
Indiana Review: "In the Deep, Deep Woods on a Dark, Dark Night."
Knocking at the Door: Poems about Approaching the Other Anthology (Write Bloody Publishing): "I Write You With the Intention of Amendment."
Literary Mama: "Wild Flower or Faded Wreath."
The Marlboro Review: "Evening Service," "The Harvest."
Mid-American Review: "Noun : Adjective : Idiom : Verb."
Migrations and Home: The Elements of Place Anthology (NatureCulture): "Bare."
Parabola, Thomas Merton Prize in Poetry of the Sacred (Honorable Mention): "Poem for the Fourth Child."
Poetry City, USA: "Triptych Depicting an Average Morning, Miracles, and the Corpse."
Radius: "Holding."
The Rutherford Red Wheelbarrow: "As the Apple Passes to Lilac," "White Grandfather Feathers and Inner Secondary Bone."
So To Speak: "If Your Family Owned a Mausoleum, then This Poem Would Make More Sense," "Self Portrait with Hand Study and Jung's Word Association Test."
Sou'wester: "Today: Kinetic."
THRUSH Poetry Journal: "Father Sings for Supper and Severance."
Tygerburning Literary Journal: "Hinge."

Writing the Land: Windblown I Anthology (NatureCulture/Human Error Publishing): "After the Prescribed Fire," "The Threshing Floor."

"Evening Service" and "The Harvest" also appear in *Lingering in the Margins: A River City Poets Anthology* (Chop Suey Books).

"Holding" was also nominated for inclusion in *Best Indie Lit New England 2012*.

"Homestead" also appears on the New Hampshire Poets Showcase website (www.nh.gov/nharts) selected by Walter E. Butts, New Hampshire Poet Laureate 2009-2013 (2014), and in the anthology *Poet Showcase: An Anthology of New Hampshire Poets* (Hobblebush Books).

"In the Deep, Deep Woods on a Dark, Dark Night" also appears on the *Indiana Review*'s Bluecast (www.soundcloud.com/inreview).

"Mirror, Mirror" was also selected for inclusion in *Dămfĭno* Press' inaugural launch of their online journal.

"There's a Third Eye to Every Memory" (Parts I-III), "The Mother, Bird," "White Grandfather Feathers and Inner Secondary Bone," "In the Deep, Deep Woods on a Dark, Dark Night," and "Noun : Adjective : Idiom : Verb" also appear in the solicited chapbook series, *5 Poems* (*Dămfĭno* Press, Five Poems Series, Book 3).

Gratitudes

I am extremely thankful for all my poetry teachers, who through the years encouraged my voice, molded my work, and pushed me to autonomy: Bruce Weigl, Eva Bourke, John F. Deane, Walter E. Butts, Neil Shepard, Paula McLain, Ira Sadoff, Ross Gay, Judith Hall, Patricia Smith, Gerald Stern, Anne Marie Macari, and Anne Waldman.

The poems collected herein have been hewn by the following writing groups, full of dear friends: The Shit House Rats, Poets Unbound, Wild Words, Tapestry of Voices/Stone Soup Poets, The Worcester Crew, The Prozac Poets (I still have *the* Pen), The Red Wheelbarrow Writers and The River City Poets. From those groups, an extra heartfelt thank you to Gary Rafferty, for starting me on this journey; Tara Bray for raising up fledgling drafts to poems; Terry Lucas for keeping this manuscript in order; and Joanna Lee, for never giving up on my writing or me…the miles and margaritas are calling, friend.

Much thanksgiving for my poetry sister, Tayve Neese. This book would not be in the world if it were not for your steadfast belief in my poems. It is a rare gift in the literary community when one of my writing heroes is also a true, dear friend, who has lent countless hours to this manuscript. Thank you, with roots deep in the fields.

These gratitudes lead to the ultimate appreciate and praise for Natasha Kane, my Editor, who has navigated this editorial process with me, with the utmost grace, compassion, and eagle eyes! Four Fields is better than it started because of you, as am I. Love you, dear one!

Last to all the amazing folks at Trio House Press, who with good care and compassion created a stunning artifact that I am deeply proud of. And to Scott and Emma, always, I love you both.

About the Author

Dorinda Wegener is a Perianesthesia Certified Registered Nurse in Richmond, VA, where she resides with her family. Wegener has had work published in many journals, including *Indiana Review, THRUSH, Hunger Mountain Review, Hayden's Ferry Review,* and *Berkeley Poetry Review*, as well as within *Poet Showcase: An Anthology of New Hampshire Poets* (Hobblebush Books) and *Lingering in the Margins: A River City Poets Anthology* (Chop Suey Books). *Four Fields* is her debut poetry collection.

About the Book

Four Fields was designed at Trio House Press through the collaboration of:

Natasha Kane, Primary Editor
Ali Shafer, Supporting Editor
Joel W. Coggins, Cover Design
Hadley Hendrix, Interior Design

The text is set in Adobe Caslon Pro.

About the Press

Trio House Press is an independent literary press dedicated to discovering, publishing, and promoting books that enhance culture and the human experience. Trio House Press adheres to and supports all ethical standards and guidelines outlined by the CLMP. For further information, or to consider making a donation to Trio House Press, visit us online at triohousepress.org.

www.ingramcontent.com/pod-product-compliance
Lightning Source LLC
Chambersburg PA
CBHW060537080526
44586CB00012B/777